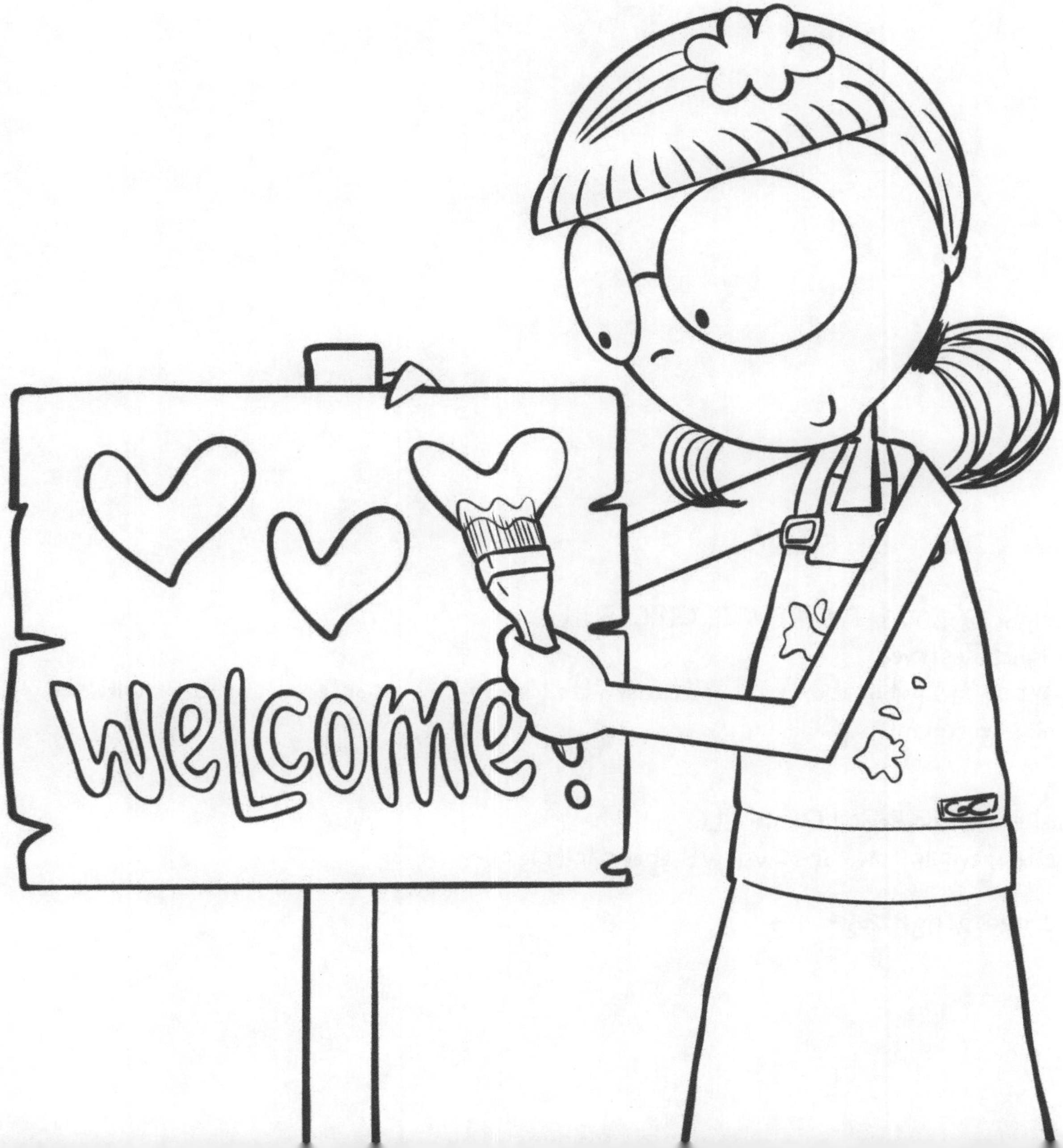

WELCOME

Let
your
colorful journey
with Flora
begin
!

Color inside, outside, around, and on top of the lines!
Use your favorite coloring tools
or experiment new techniques and mix up different media!

Whether you are young or adult,
an outdoor enthusiast or simply looking for relaxing time,
this book is going to be a fun opportunity
to let your creativity flow
and fully engage in the present moment.

Dive into the activity by yourself
or share the experience with friends and family...
fantastic adventures are waiting for you!

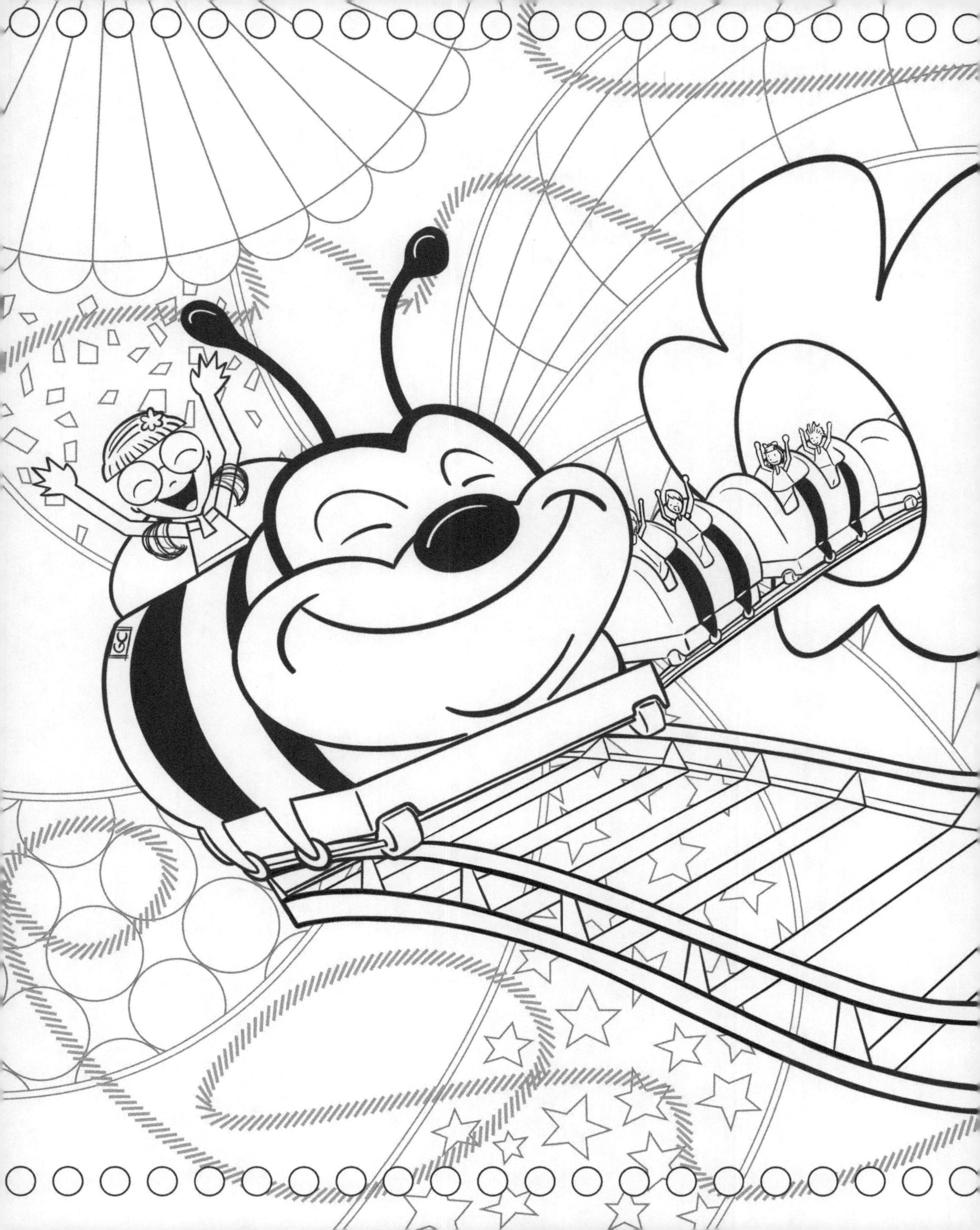

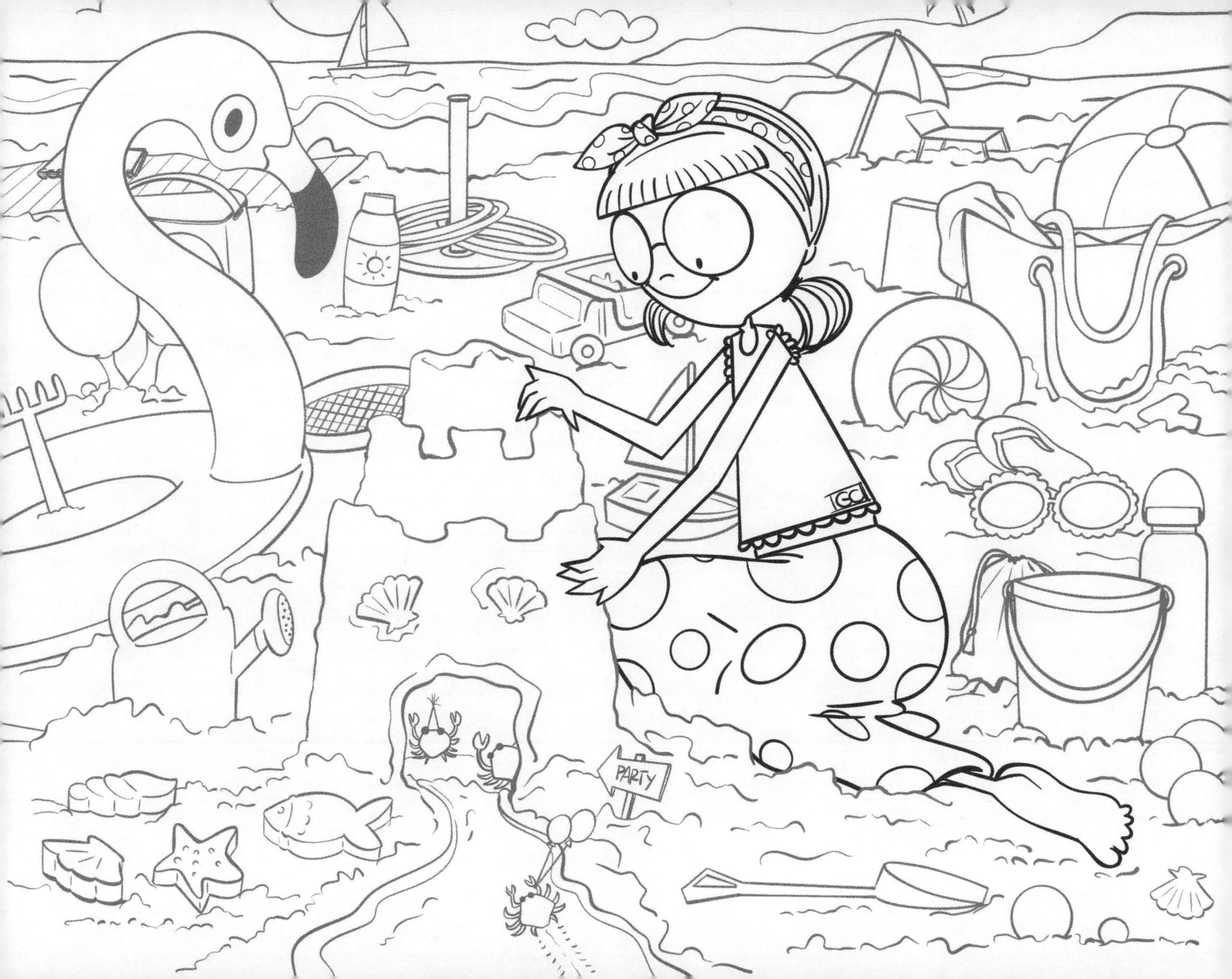
PARTY

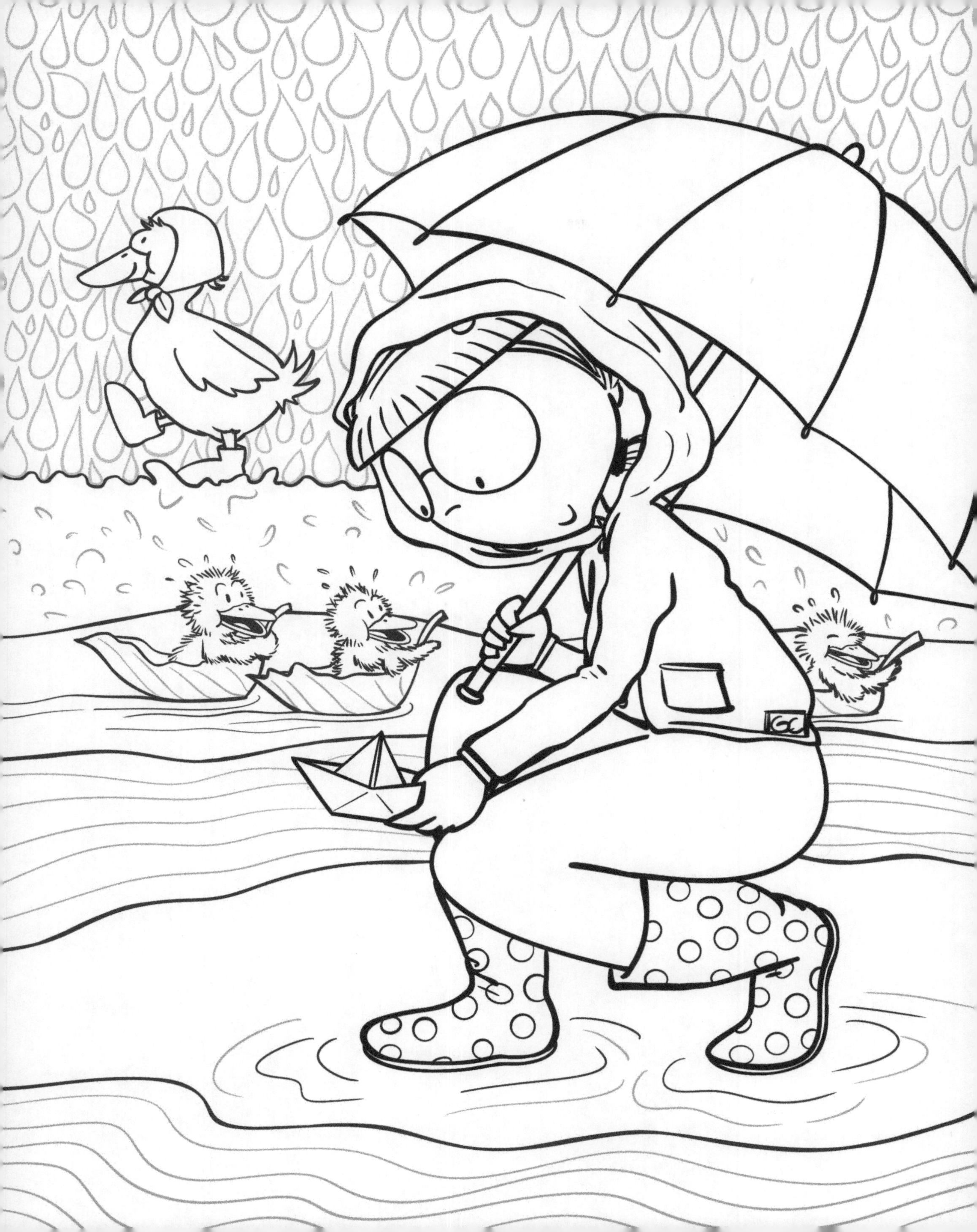

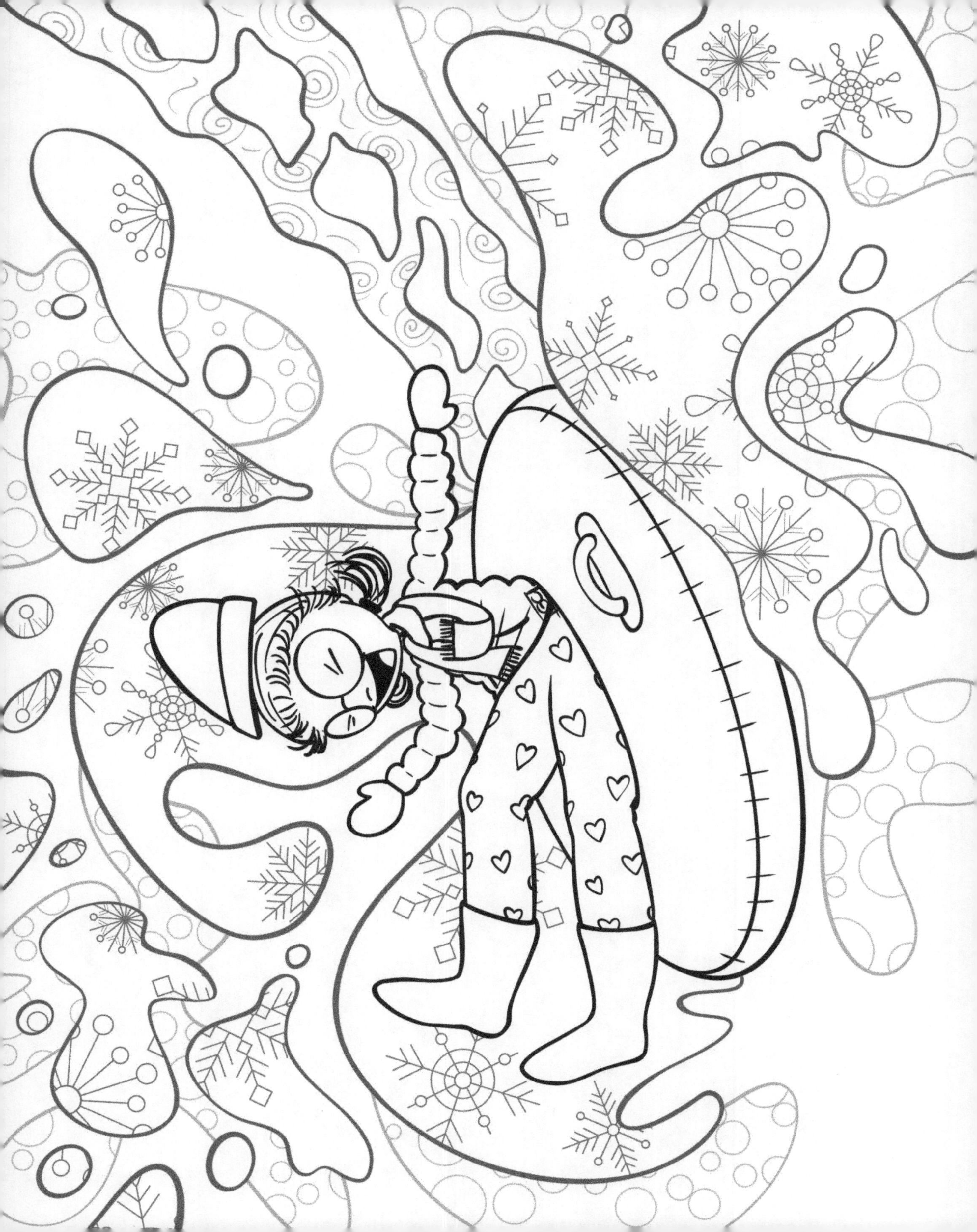

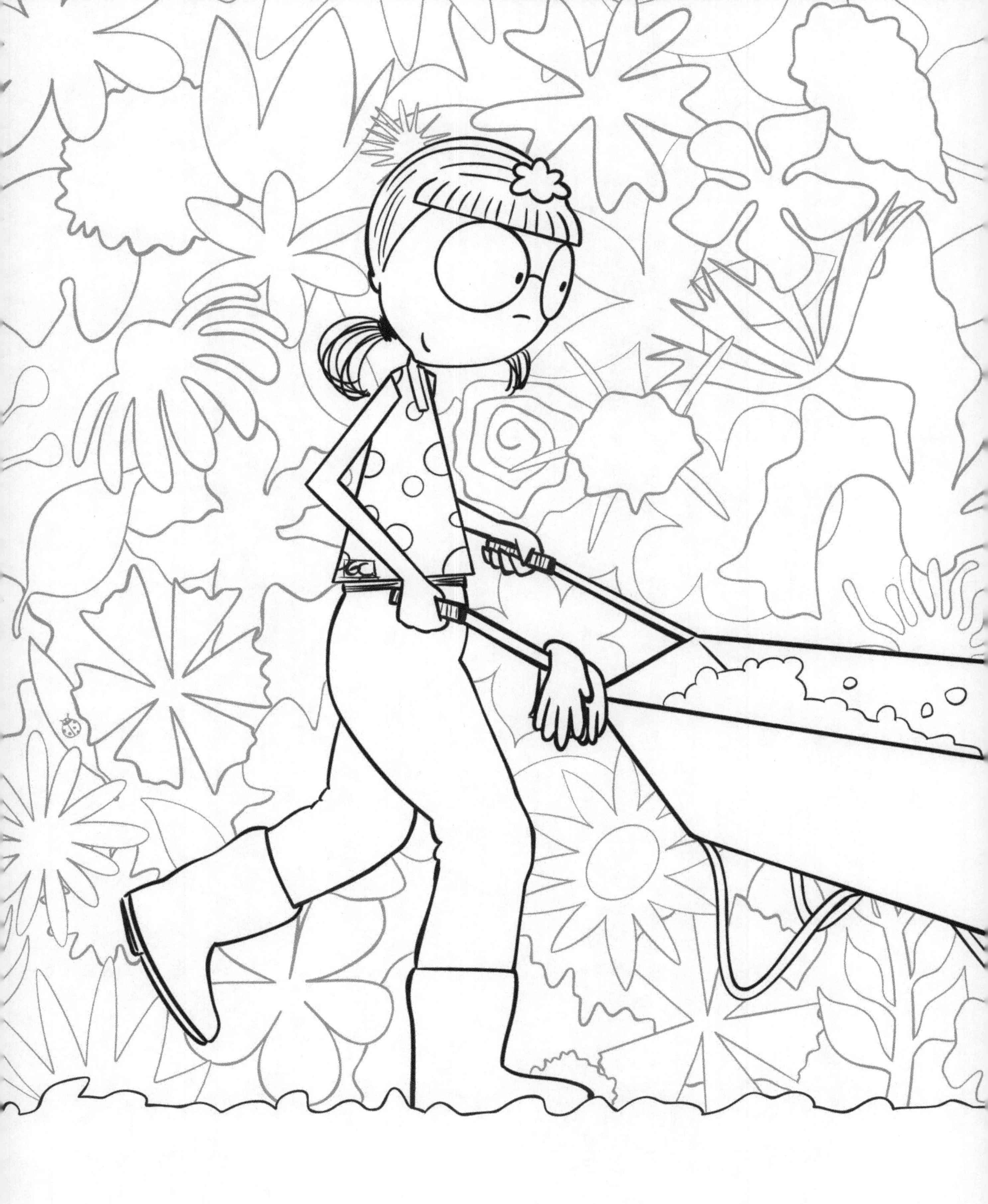

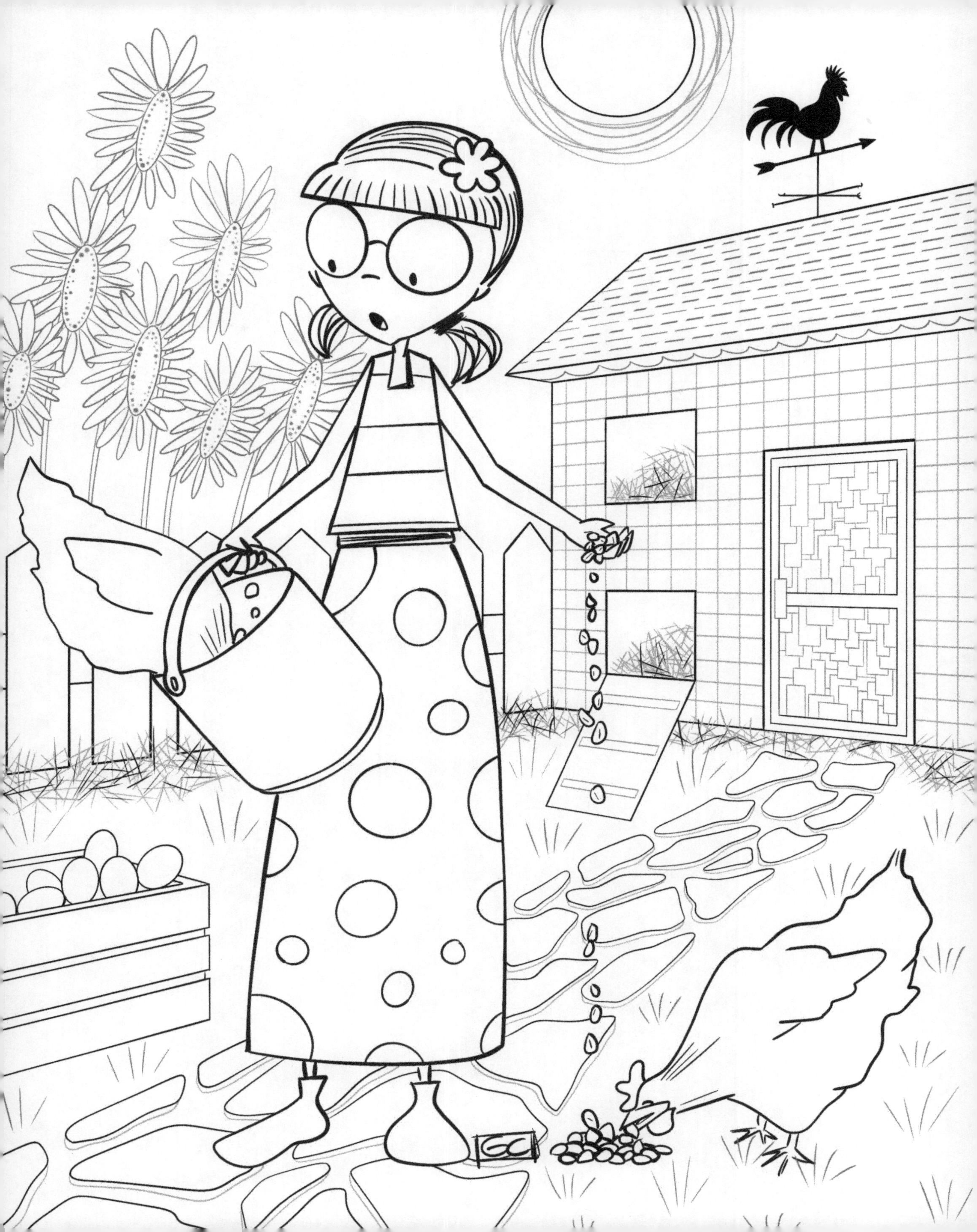

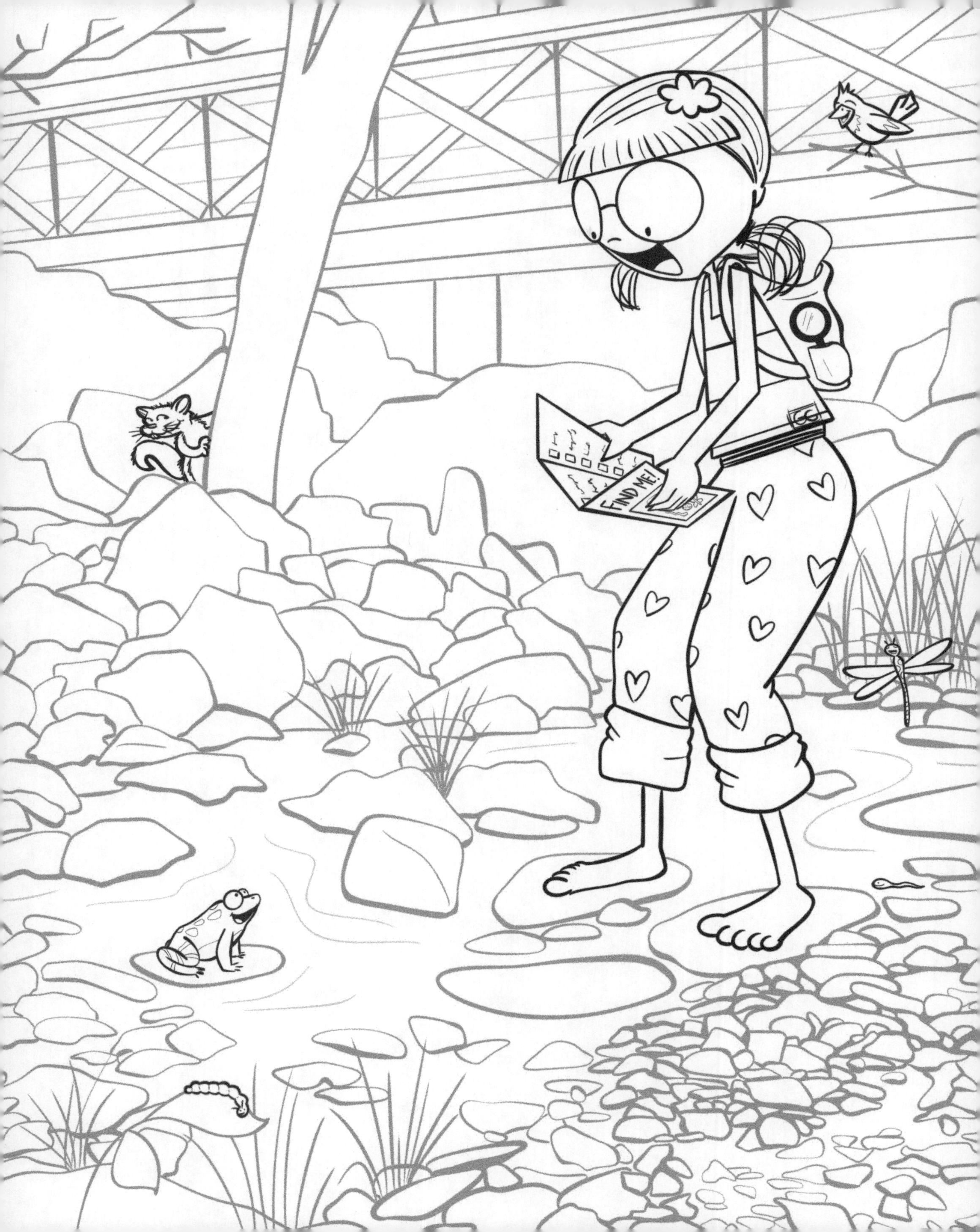

FIND ME!

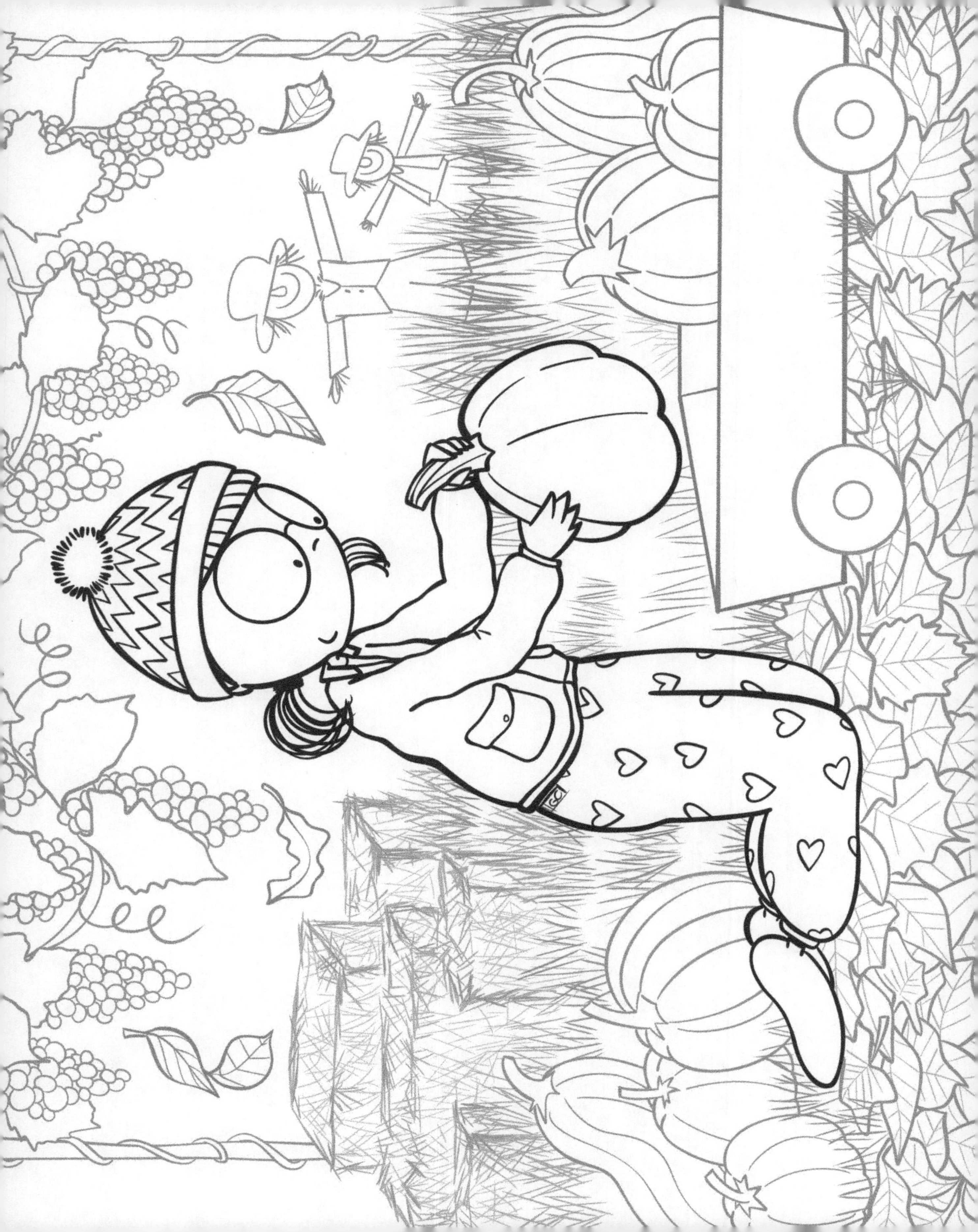

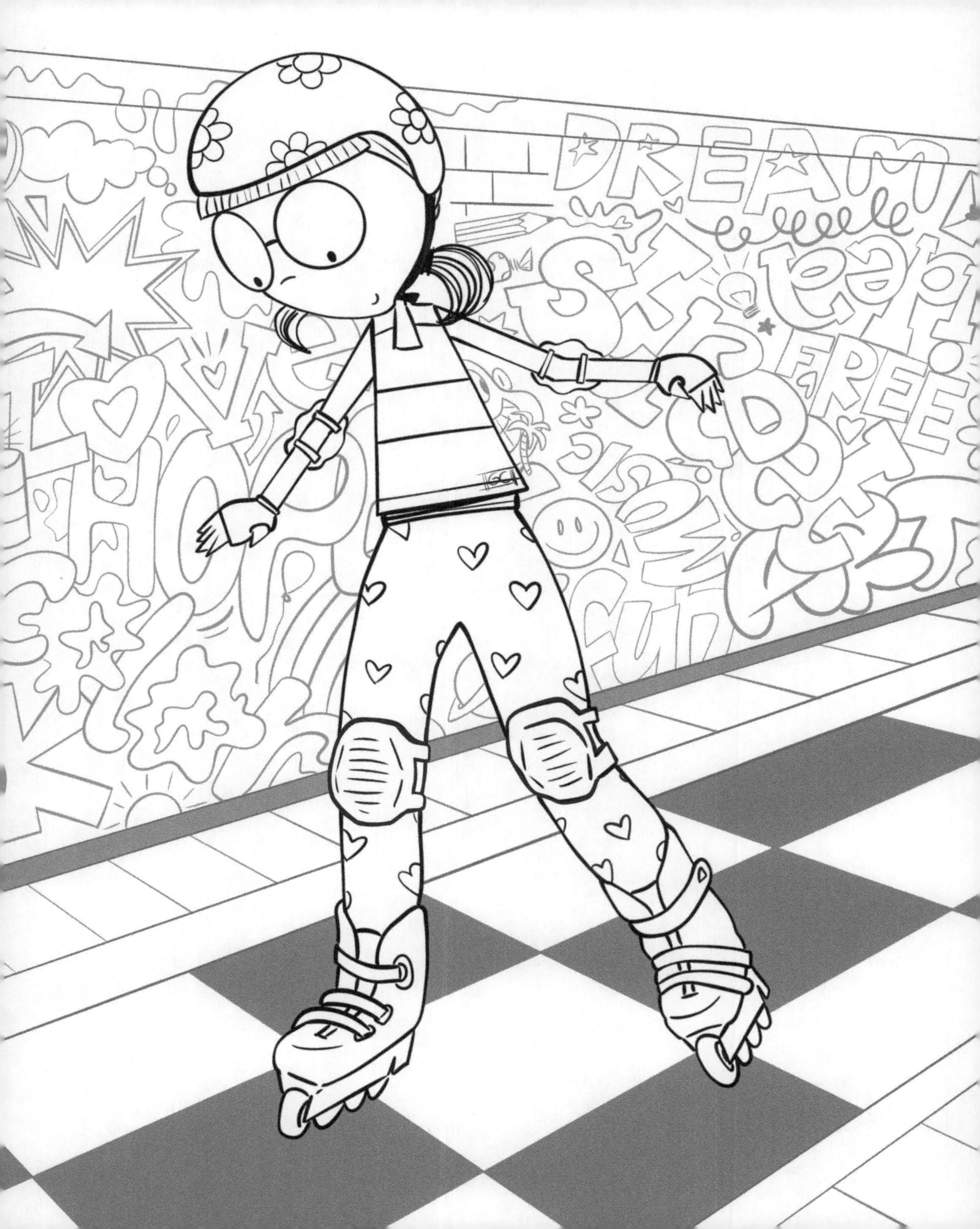

DREAM
SK8
FREE

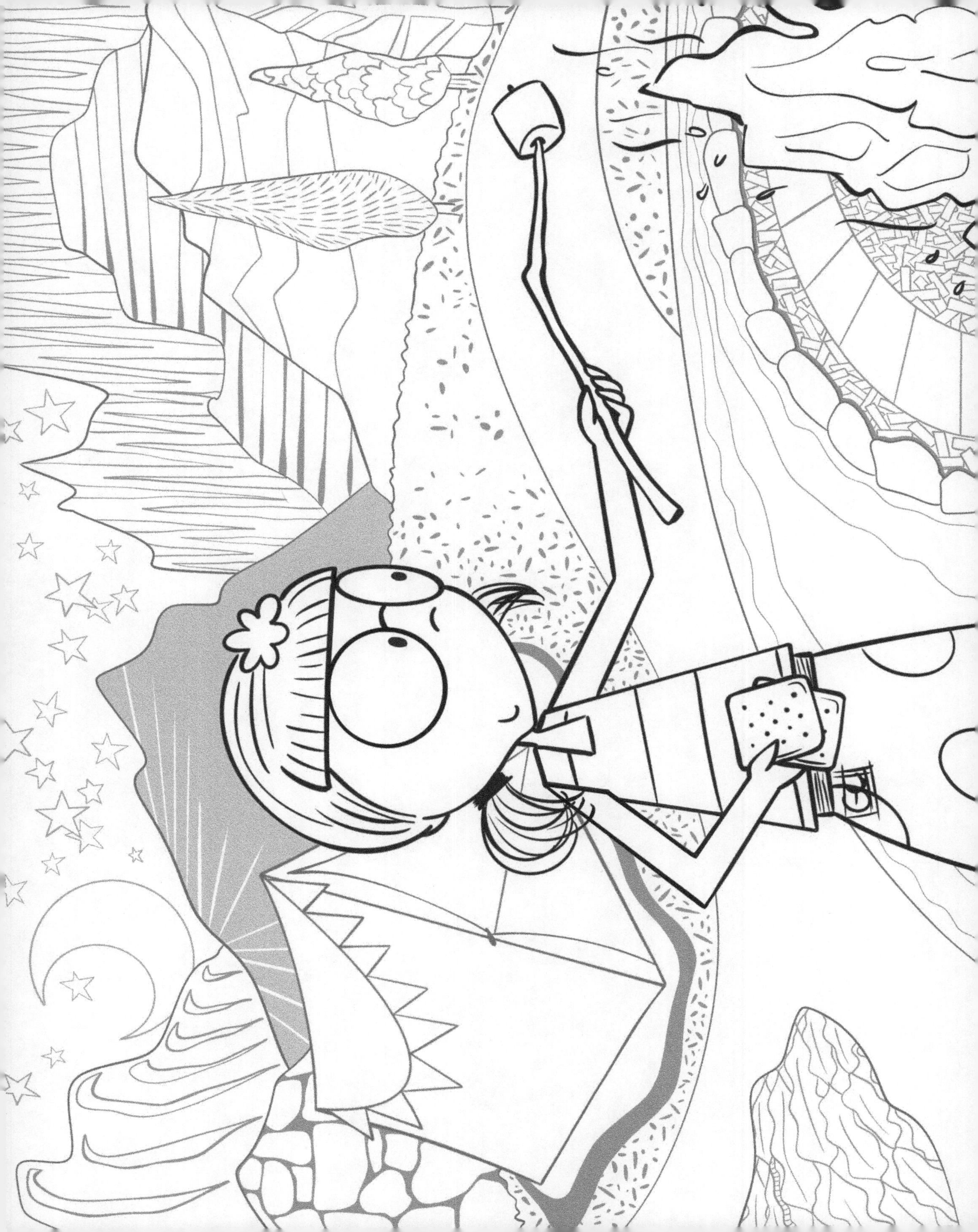

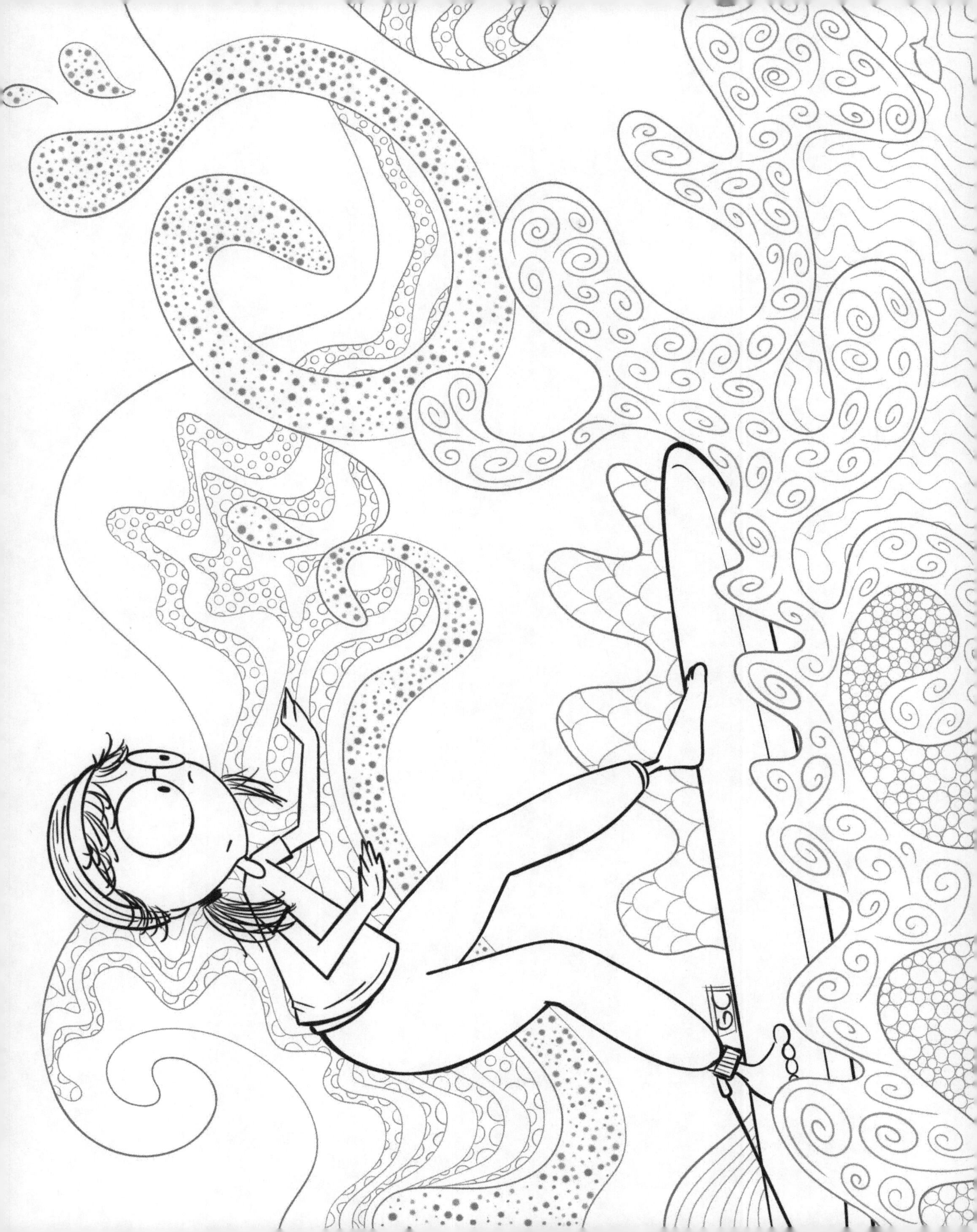

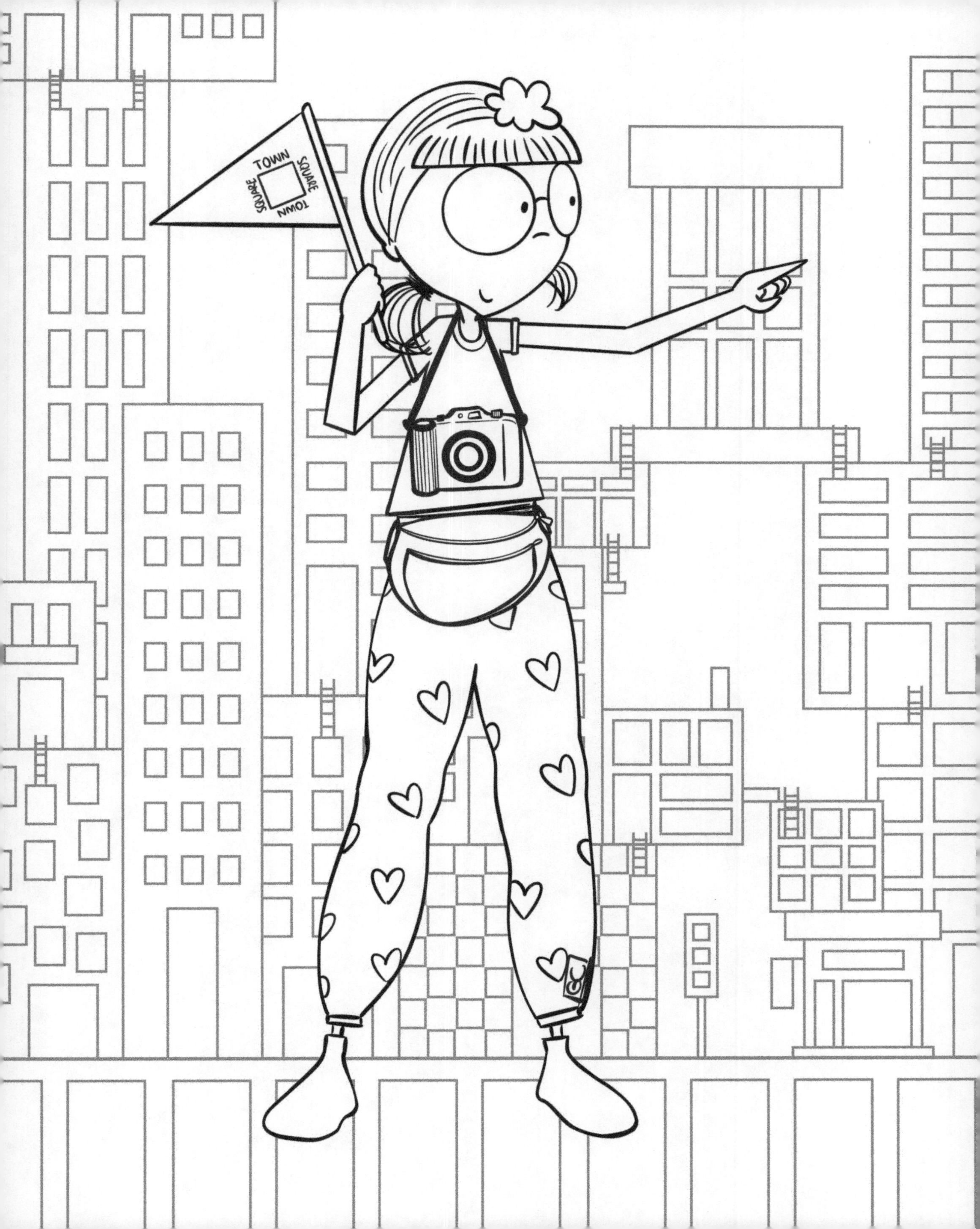

TOWN SQUARE
TOWN SQUARE

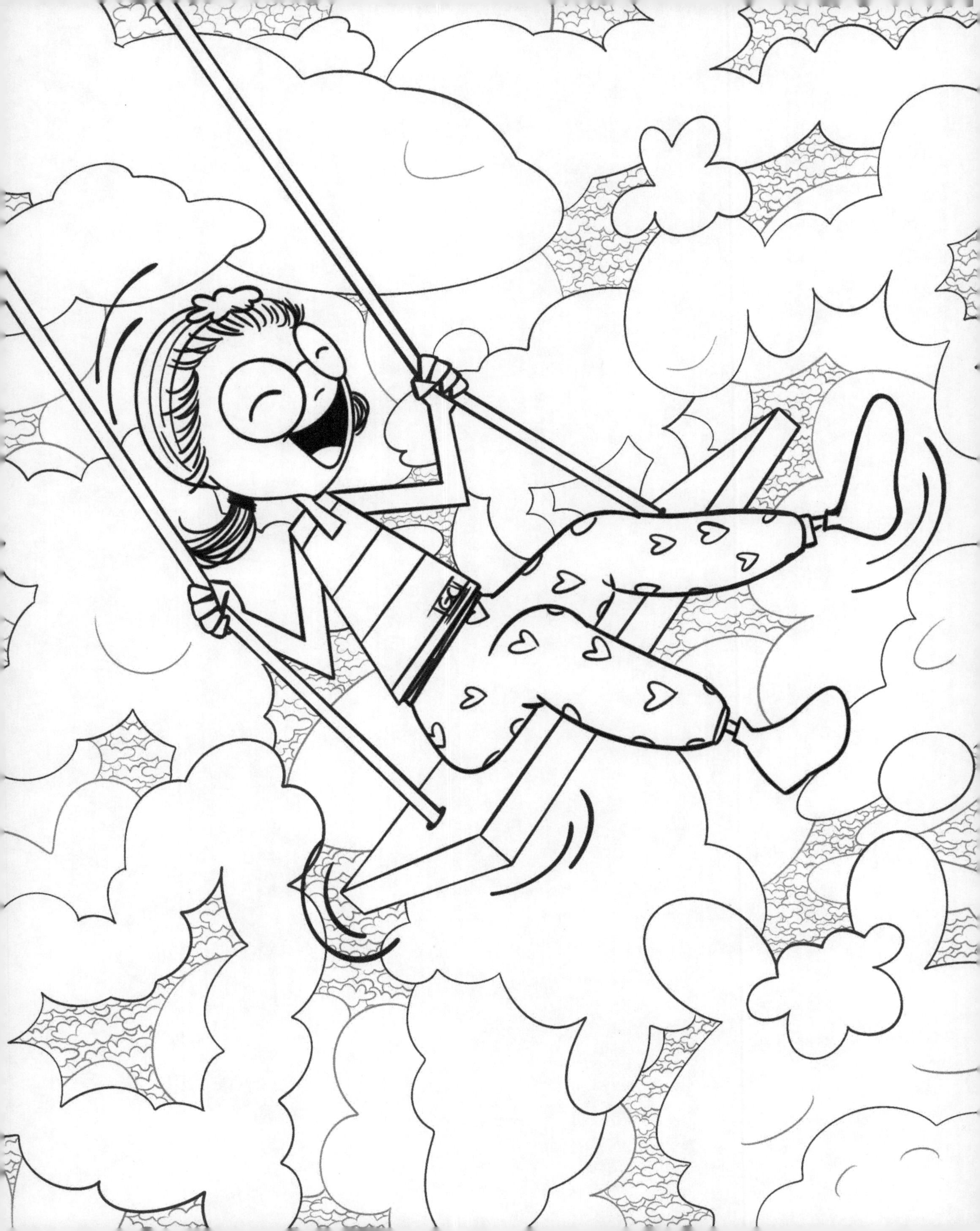

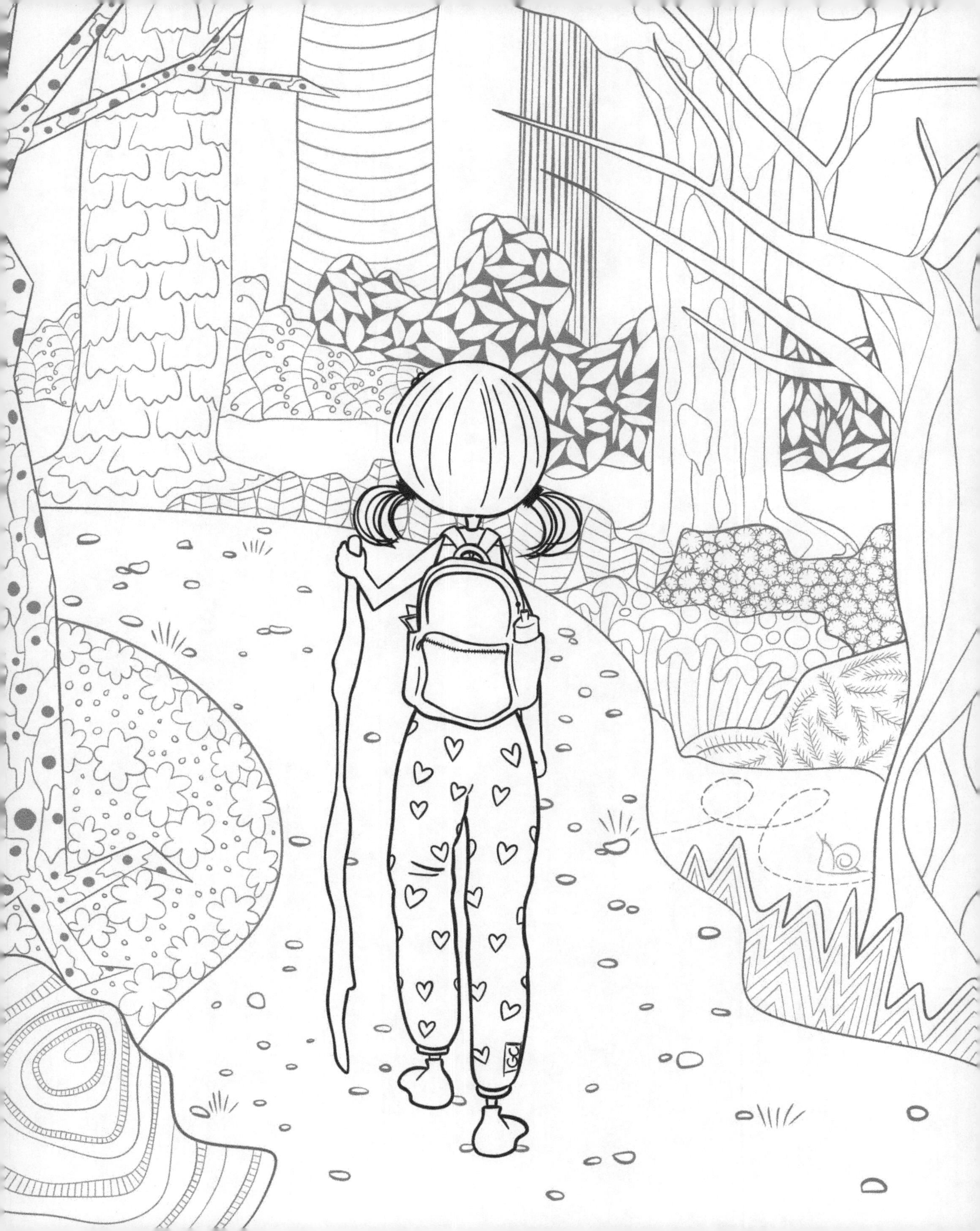

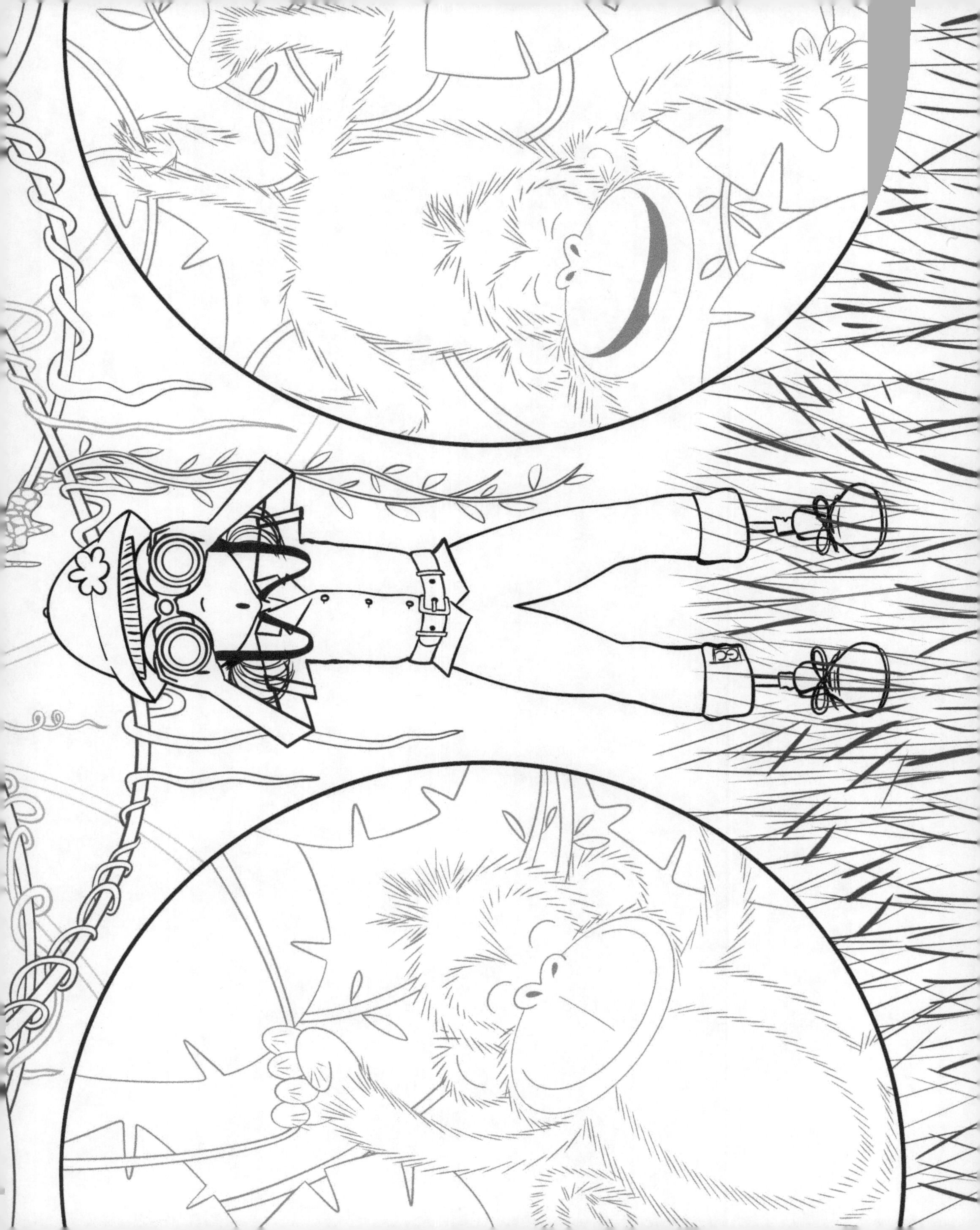

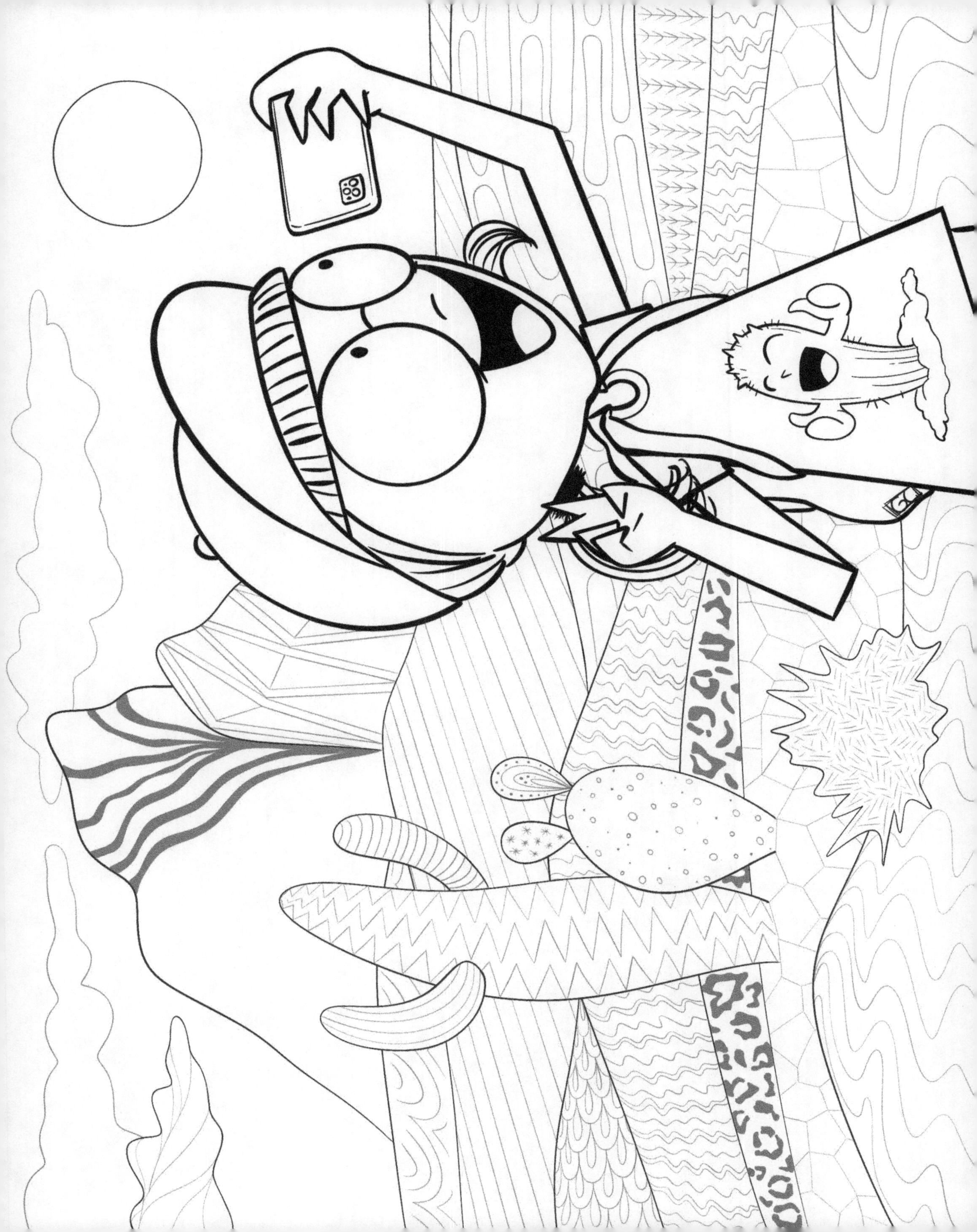

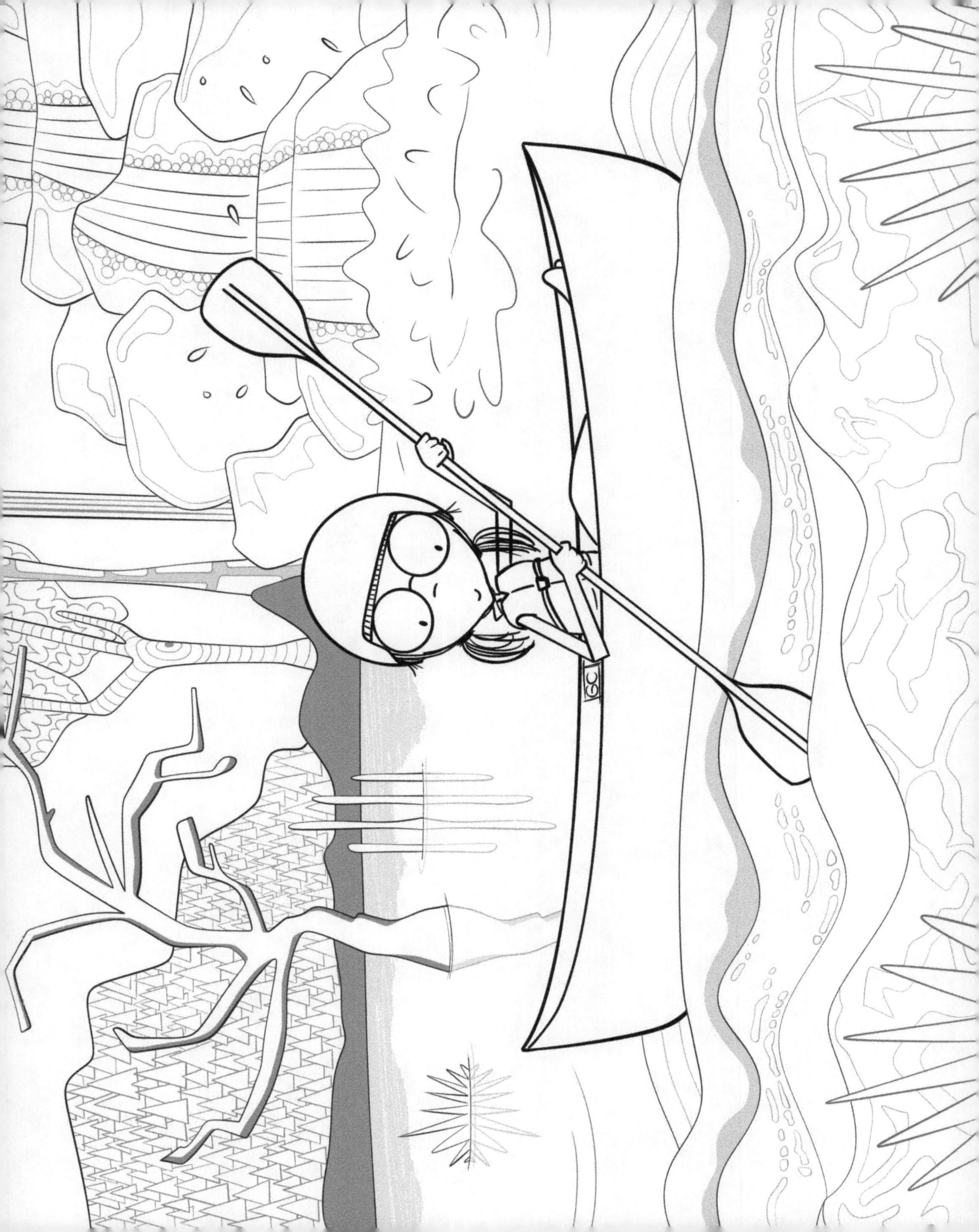

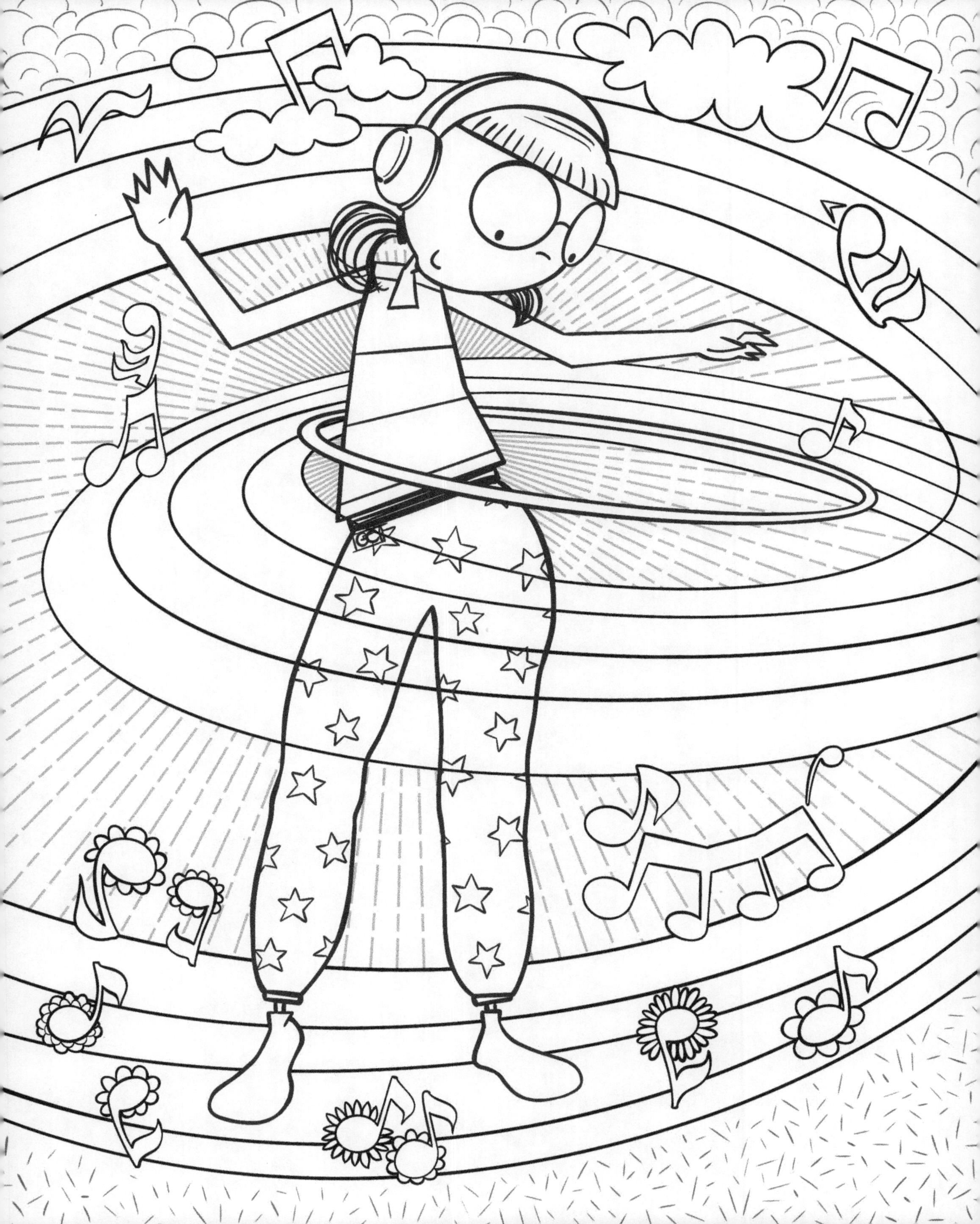

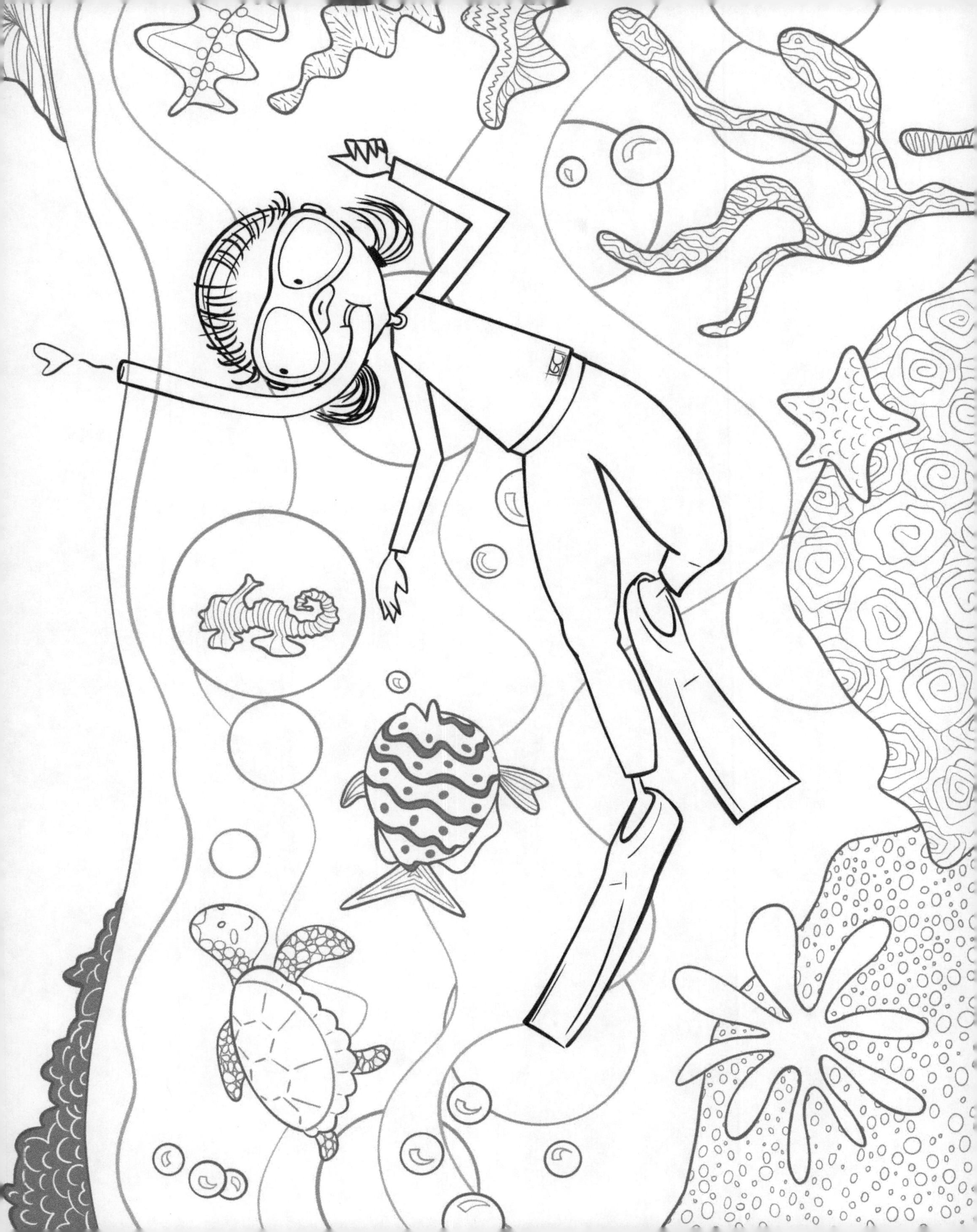

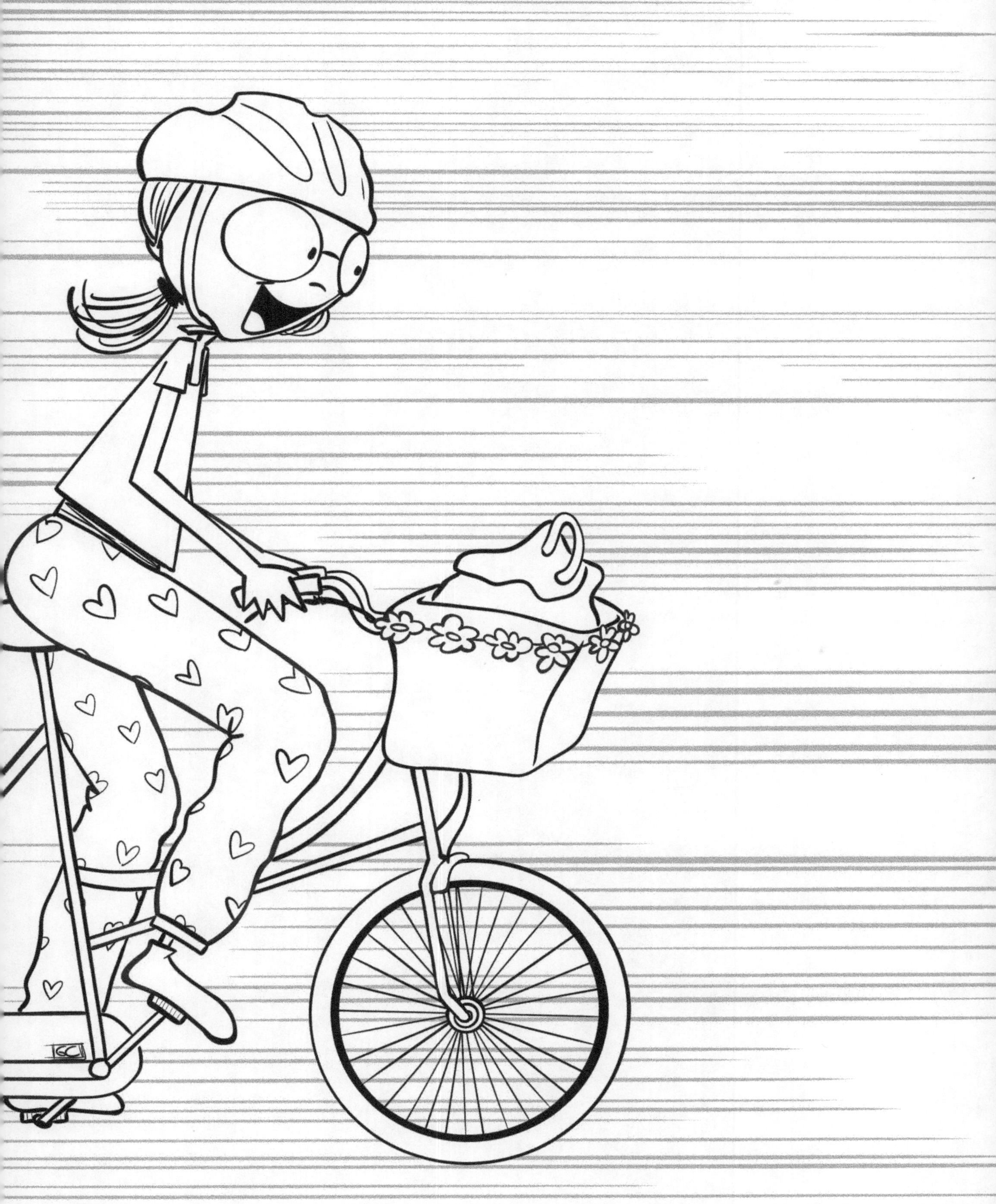

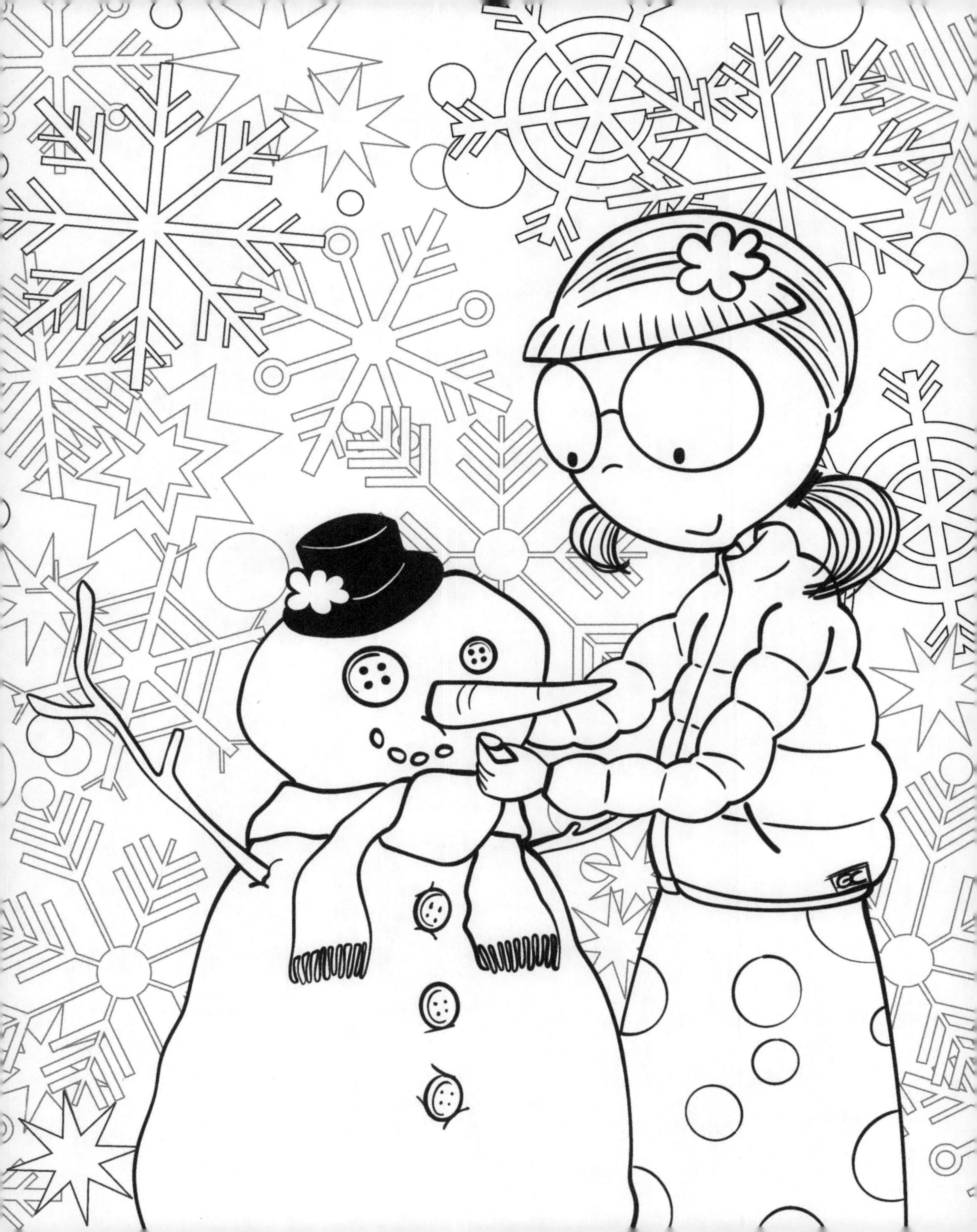

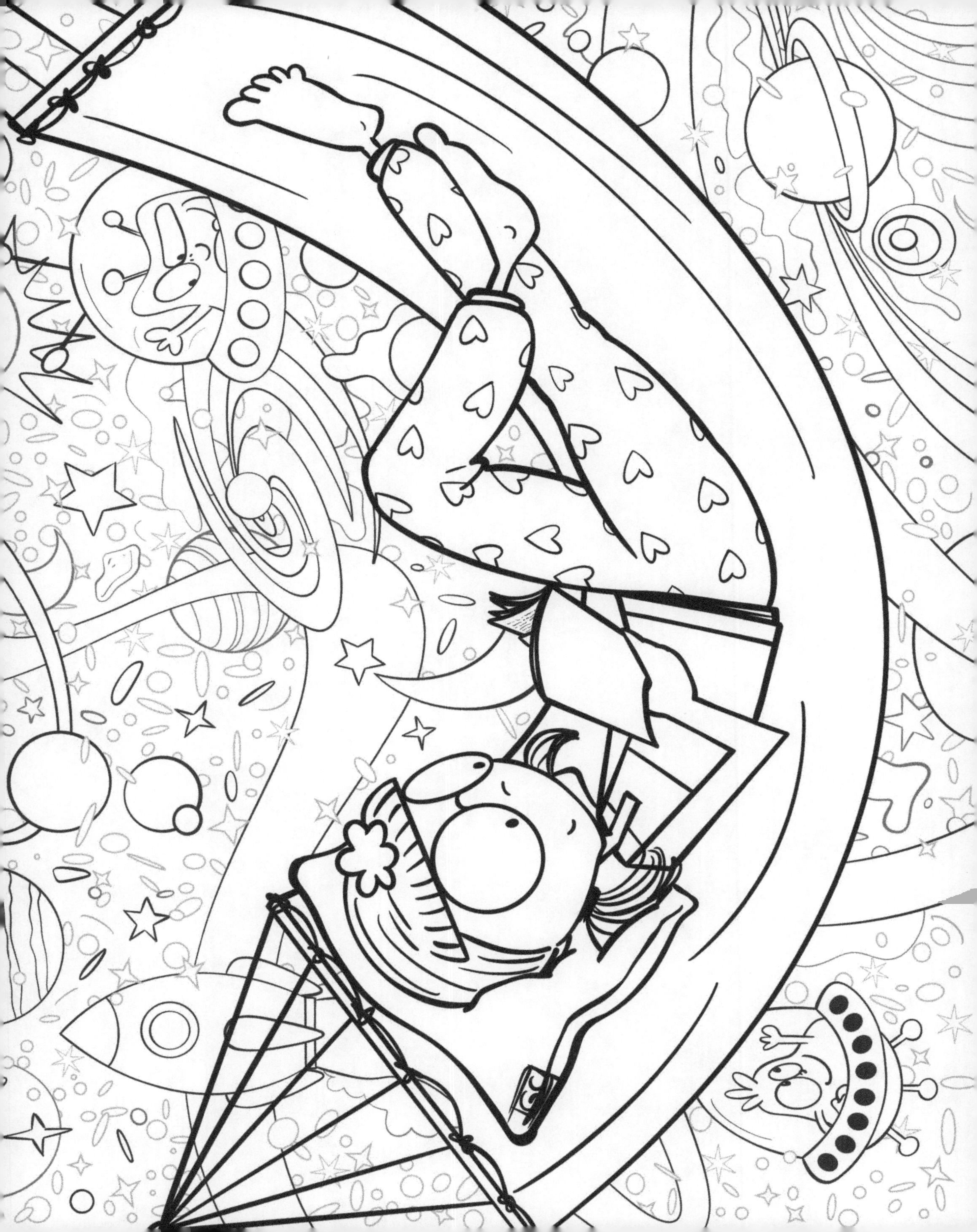

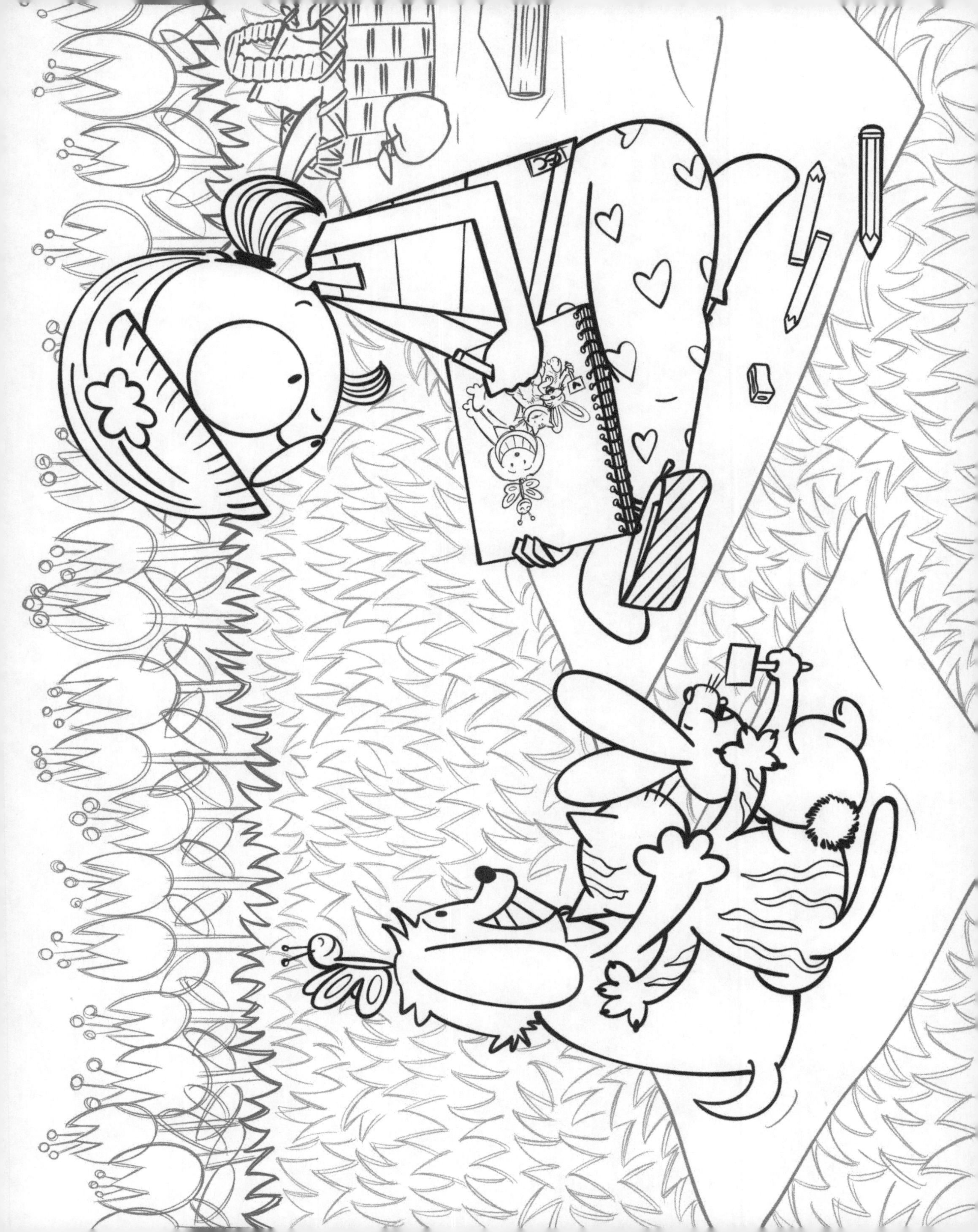

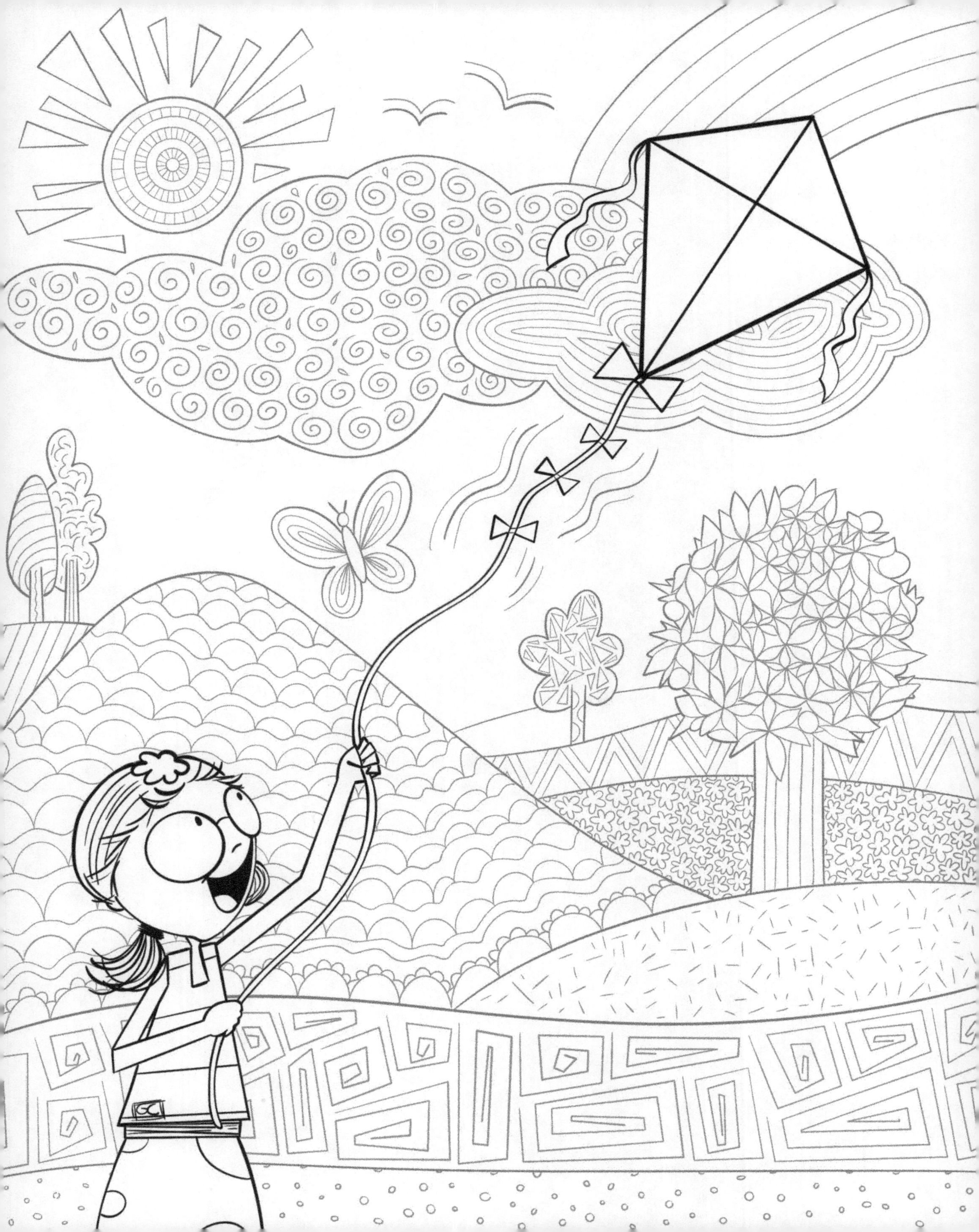

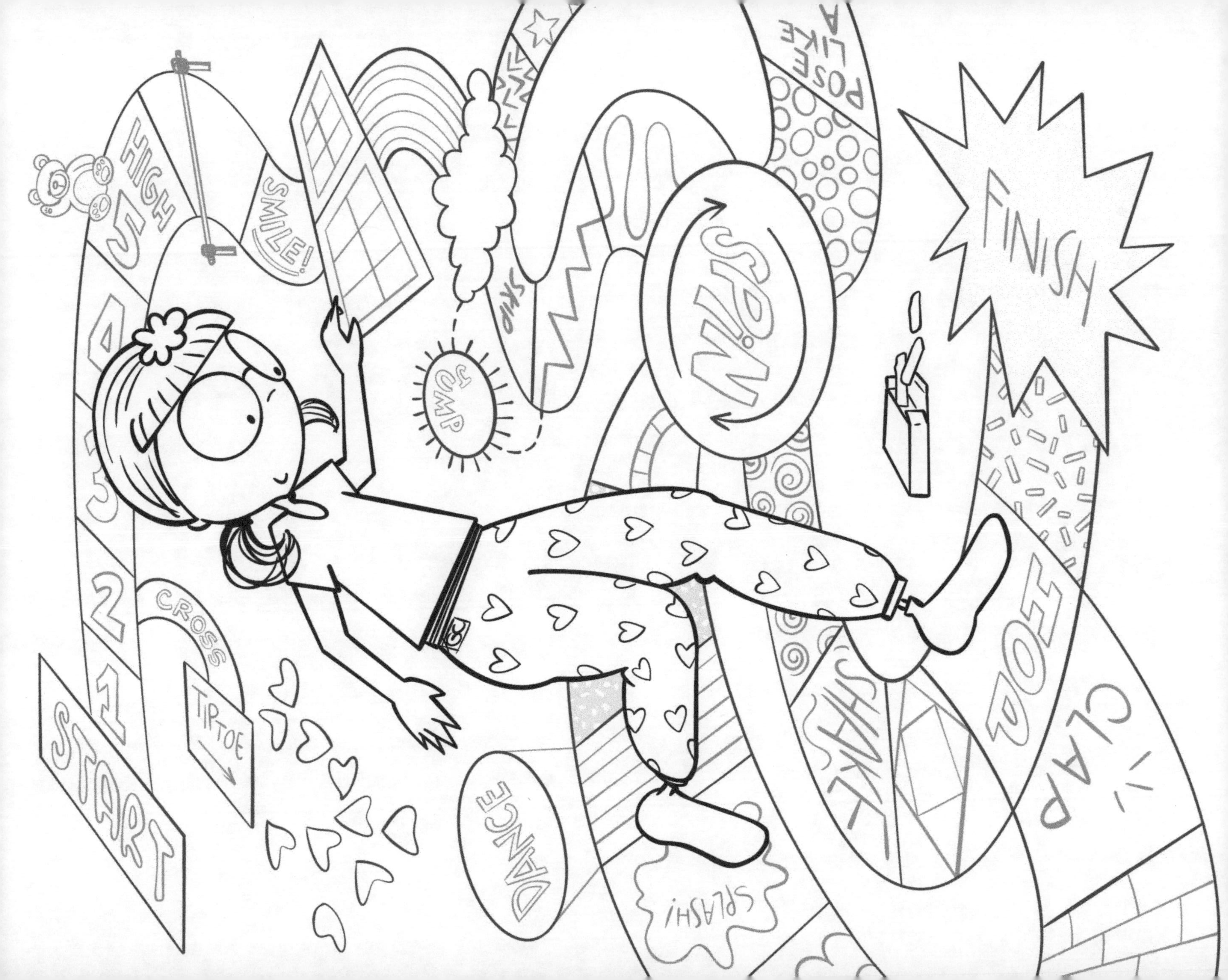

START
1
2
3
TIPTOE
CROSS
HIGH
SMILE!
SKIP
DANCE
SPLASH!
JUMP
SPIN
CLAP
SHAKE
HOP
POSE LIKE
FINISH

Dear Friend, I hope you had fun coloring with Flora!

THANK YOU!!!!!
I can't wait to hear from you!

Send your thoughts, comments, and feedback to flora@floramakesmesmile.com!

If you enjoyed the book, please consider leaving a **review** wherever you bought it from! Your help in spreading the word does make a difference!

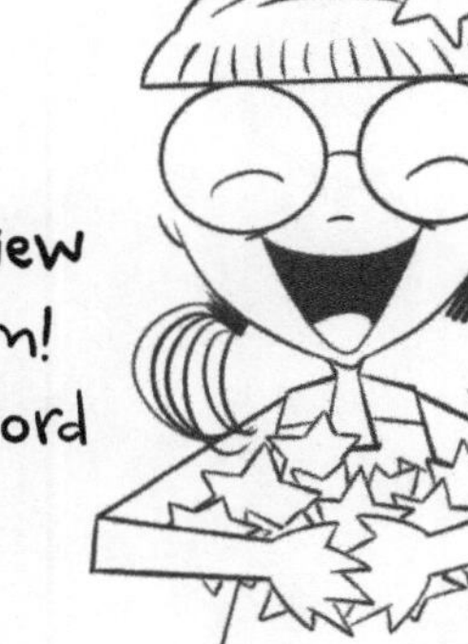

Share your works of art on social media using the hashtag #floramakesmesmile! I would love to see your finished pages!!!

(to all friends under 18 years old, ask your grown-up for permission before posting your photos!)

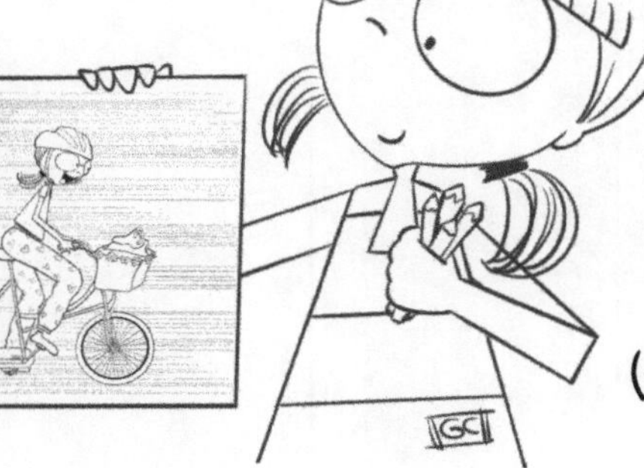

Do you want more art activities? Check out the book 'Think, Sketch, and Smile with Flora'! A collection of 50 fun worksheets is ready for you!

Follow Flora's adventures!!!
www.floramakesmesmile.com
FACEBOOK: @floramakesmesmile
INSTAGRAM: @flora_makes_me_smile